KU-350-461

A. Roy

my first book of
questions and answers

simple science

Rosie Greenwood

p

This is a Parragon Book
This edition published in 2003

Parragon
Queen Street House
4 Queen Street
Bath BA1 1HE, UK

Copyright © Parragon 2001

Produced by

David West ☗ Children's Books
7 Princeton Court
55 Felsham Road
Putney
London SW15 1AZ

All rights reserved. No part of this publication may be reproduced, stored in a retrieval system, or transmitted by any means, electronic, mechanical, photocopying, recording or otherwise, without the prior permission of the copyright holder.

British Library Cataloguing-in-Publication Data

A catalogue record for this book is available from the British Library.

ISBN 0-75259-827-9

Printed in China

Designers
Aarti Parmar, Rob Shone, Fiona Thorne

Illustrator
Janie Perie (Allied Artists)

Cartoonist
Peter Wilks (SGA)

Editor
James Pickering

CONTENTS

? What is air made of?

Air is a mixture of invisible gases.
The main ones are nitrogen and
oxygen, but there's also some carbon
dioxide, water vapour and other gases,
as well as tiny bits of salt, dust and dirt.

? How do we know air is there?

We can't see or taste or smell air,
but we can feel and hear it when
the wind blows. Wind is moving
air – it's what makes trees bend
and leaves rustle, and what blows
sailing boats across the water.

? *Is there air in Space?*

The skin of air around the Earth is called the atmosphere, and it fades away into nothingness at about 500 km above the ground – that's where Space begins. There's no air in Space, but most of the other planets have their own atmospheres.

TRUE OR FALSE?

We need to breathe air to live.

TRUE. Humans and all other animals would die without the gas oxygen.

There's air on Mars.

TRUE. But carbon dioxide is the main gas in Mars's atmosphere, and there's not enough oxygen to keep us alive.

? Where does water go when puddles dry out?

Water does a magical trick when it gets very hot – it becomes invisible! When it bakes in the Sun's heat, it changes into the invisible gas water vapour and floats away in the air.

? What is steam?

When water vapour hits something cold, it cools and starts to change back from an invisible gas into a liquid. We can see steam because it's made up of masses of tiny droplets of liquid water.

❓ *Where does ice come from?*

Ice is what happens when water gets very, very cold – it freezes into a solid. Most materials will change from a liquid into a gas if they get hot enough, and from a liquid into a solid if they get cold enough.

Your body is mainly water.

TRUE. About 65% of your body is water. Elephants are 70% water and worms are 80%.

Icebergs can be as big as skyscrapers.

TRUE. Believe it or not, the tallest iceberg ever seen was well over 150 m high!

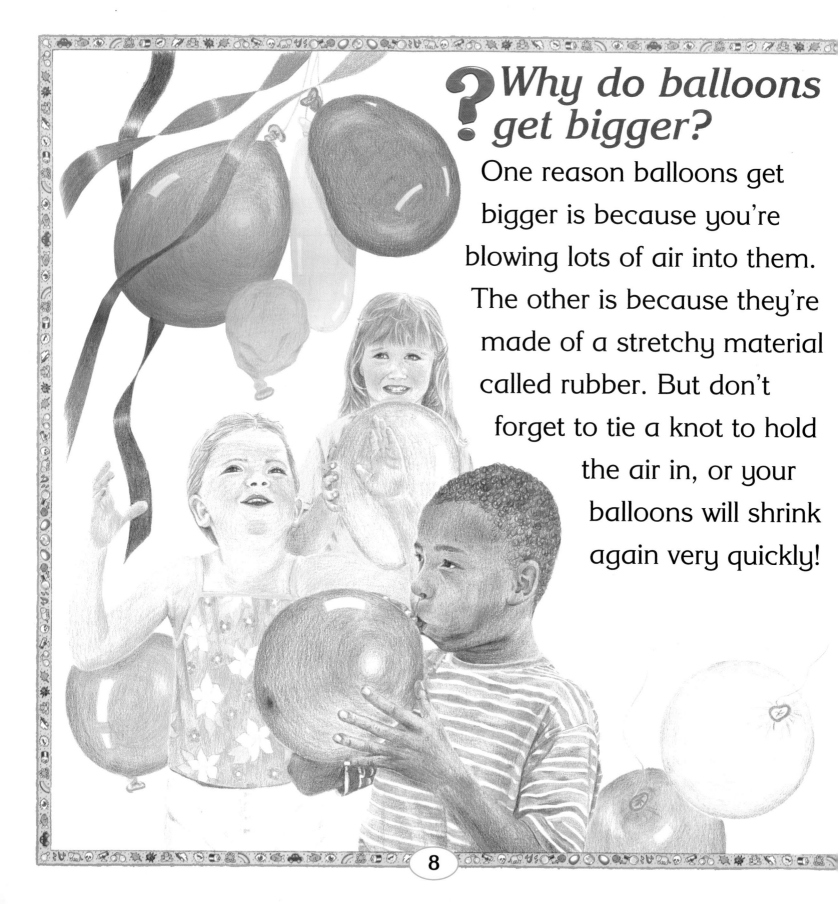

? *Why do balloons get bigger?*

One reason balloons get bigger is because you're blowing lots of air into them. The other is because they're made of a stretchy material called rubber. But don't forget to tie a knot to hold the air in, or your balloons will shrink again very quickly!

?Why do balloons float?

Things float upwards when they're lighter than their surroundings. Air-filled balloons are roughly the same weight as the air around them, which is why they don't float all that well. The best floaters are filled with a gas that's much lighter than air. It's called helium, and it's used in airships as well as in party balloons.

TRUE OR FALSE?

You cannot weigh air.

FALSE. Like everything on Earth, air has weight – 4,000 balloons would weigh the same as a tub of ice cream.

Most fish use balloons to help them float.

TRUE. Most fish have a gas-filled bag called a swim bladder inside them, which helps them float.

❓ Why do rubber ducks float in the bath?

Air is lighter than water, and one reason a rubber duck floats is because it's stuffed full of air. The water helps, too, because it pushes up on the duck. This upwards push is called upthrust.

❓ Why does the water level rise when I get in the bath?

When you get in the bath, your body pushes the water out of the way. The only place the water can go is up, so the water level rises.

❓ Why does the soap sink?

Things will float in water only if they are lighter than the amount of water they push aside. If they are heavier, the water's upthrust isn't strong enough to hold them up. A bar of soap will sink if it's heavier than the amount of water it pushes aside.

TRUE OR FALSE?

It's easier to float in salty water.

TRUE. Salty water has more upthrust than fresh water.

Showers are a modern invention.

FALSE. The first showers were taken as long as 2,500 years ago, by the Ancient Greeks.

? Where does sugar go in hot drinks?

Sugar doesn't just vanish in hot drinks, it does the same trick in cold ones. It doesn't completely disappear, though – you can taste it's there. You can't see the sugar, because it spreads completely into the water. We call this dissolving.

? *Why do fizzy drinks have bubbles?*

The bubbles in fizzy drinks are the gas carbon dioxide. You can't see them when the top is on the bottle because the carbon dioxide is dissolved in the water.

Lots of carbon dioxide is squashed into the drink, and when you open the bottle, the gas escapes as bubbles.

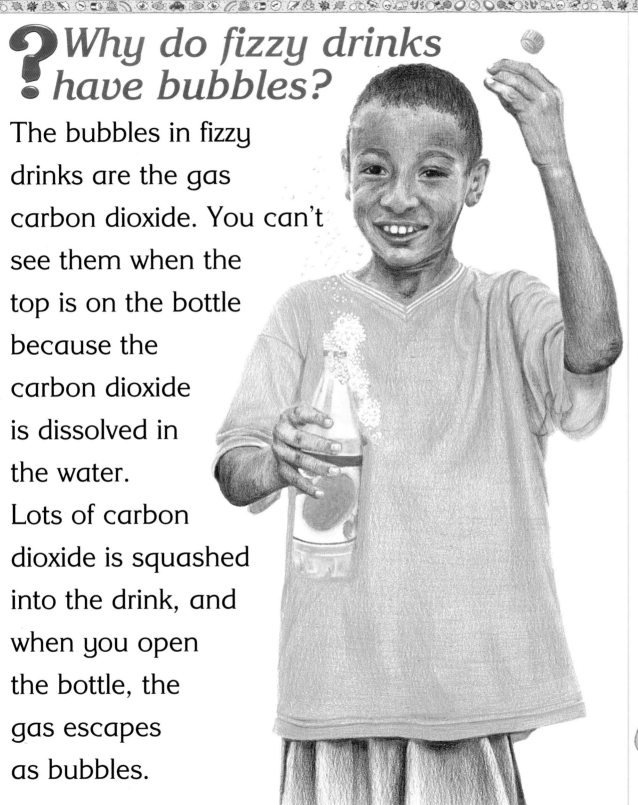

TRUE OR FALSE?

Fish breathe air just as we do.

FALSE. They breathe the oxygen dissolved in water.

Salt comes from sea water.

TRUE. It's dissolved in sea water. To separate it, sea water is heated until the water changes into gas and floats away, leaving the salt behind.

❓ *Why can't we see in the dark?*

We can't see in the dark because we can't see without light. Objects like trees and houses don't give off their own light, even in the daytime. We can only see them because sunlight is bouncing off them into our eyes. This bouncing off is called reflection.

❓ *Why can I see myself in a mirror?*

When light hits something rough like a blanket, it scatters in all directions – like spilling sugar. But when light hits something smooth like a mirror, it comes straight back – like a ball bouncing off a wall. You see yourself in a mirror because light bounces off your face towards the mirror, and then straight back into your eyes.

TRUE OR FALSE?

The Moon shines with its own light.

FALSE. Moonlight is sunshine bouncing off the Moon towards us.

Cats have mirrors in their eyes.

TRUE. Cats' eyes have a mirror-like layer to help them see in the dark.

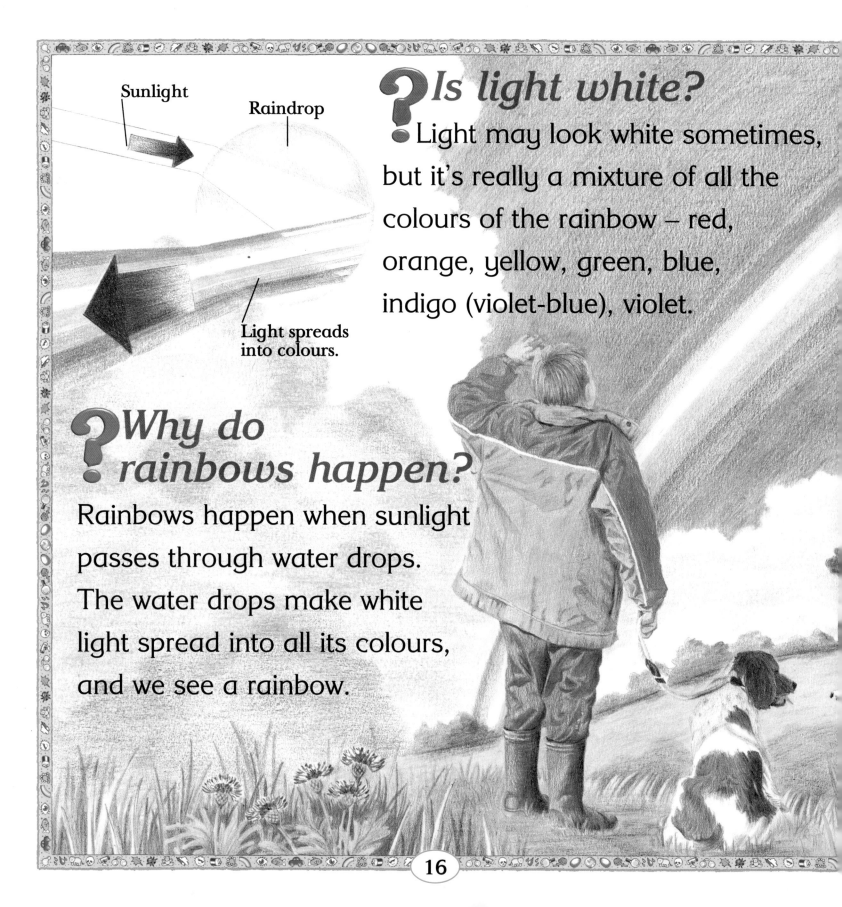

Sunlight

Raindrop

Light spreads into colours.

?Is light white?

Light may look white sometimes, but it's really a mixture of all the colours of the rainbow – red, orange, yellow, green, blue, indigo (violet-blue), violet.

?Why do rainbows happen?

Rainbows happen when sunlight passes through water drops. The water drops make white light spread into all its colours, and we see a rainbow.

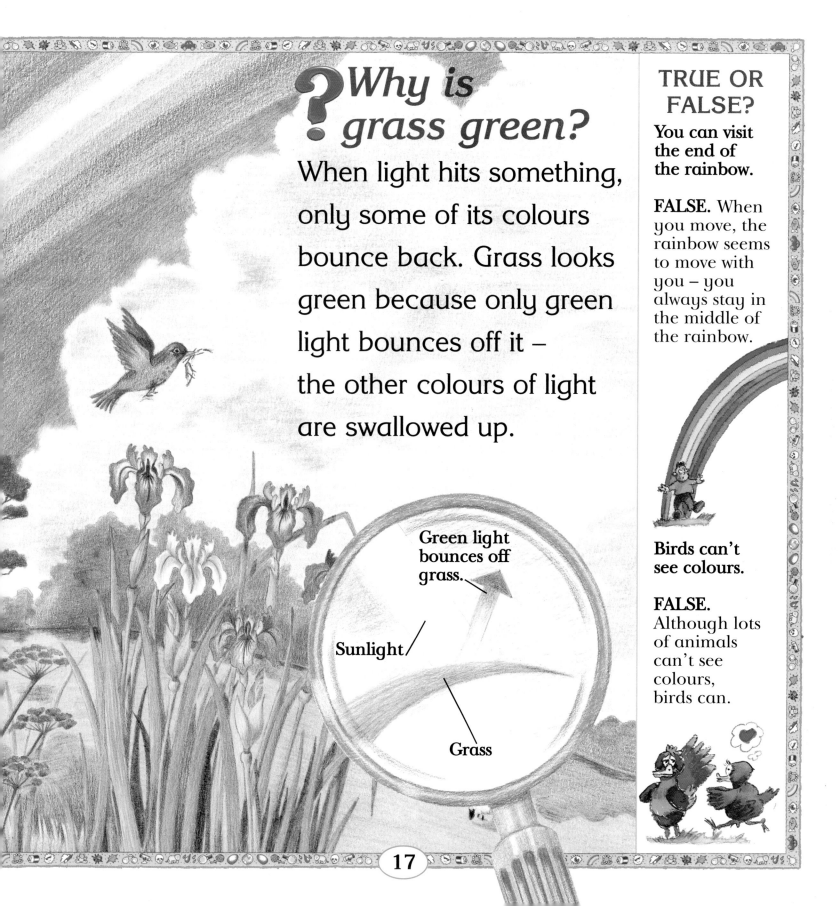

? Why is grass green?

When light hits something, only some of its colours bounce back. Grass looks green because only green light bounces off it – the other colours of light are swallowed up.

Green light bounces off grass.

Sunlight

Grass

TRUE OR FALSE?

You can visit the end of the rainbow.

FALSE. When you move, the rainbow seems to move with you – you always stay in the middle of the rainbow.

Birds can't see colours.

FALSE. Although lots of animals can't see colours, birds can.

? Why does opening the curtains make it light?

Light can pass through some materials, such as window glass, but not others. When materials let light through, we call them transparent.

? Where do shadows come from?

Your body isn't transparent, so it blocks the light and makes the dark patch we call a shadow form. You can test this out on a sunny day – to see your shadow, stand with your back to the Sun.

? Why does drawing the curtains make it dark?

When things don't let light through, we call them opaque. If curtains are made of thick, heavy cloth, they can be opaque enough to block light and make rooms dark, even during the day.

Transparent

Opaque

TRUE OR FALSE?

You can jump on your shadow.

FALSE. Your shadow moves with you.

You can tell the time with shadows.

TRUE. Shadow clocks are called sundials.

19

❓ Where does electricity come from?

Most of our electricity is made in power stations by machines called generators. Electricity is a kind of energy and it flows into our homes, schools and towns through cables buried beneath our feet or wires hanging high over our heads.

❓ Why can't we see electricity?

Electricity is made of things called electrons, which are so tiny that we can't see them.

Electricity is very very dangerous – always ask a grown-up before you use something electrical.

? *How can I make electricity?*

? You can make a safe kind of electricity by rubbing a balloon against a nylon jumper. It's called static electricity and it has pulling power – test this out by sticking the balloon on a wall.

TRUE OR FALSE?

Wind is used to make electricity.

TRUE. Electricity generators are powered by wind, water, coal, oil, gas or nuclear fuel.

Our electricity comes from the sky.

FALSE. Lightning is a flash of static electricity, but it isn't used to power things.

❓Why do things stop working when you switch them off?

Electricity only works when it can flow all the way around a loop called a circuit. Turning off a switch breaks the circuit, stopping the flow and turning electrical things like lights off. Turning a switch on joins the circuit and makes them work again.

Ask a grown-up to help you make this simple switch and circuit.

Drawing pin

Paper clips act as a switch.

22

Small torch bulb

Tape

Light bulb comes on when the switch is turned on.

Wooden base

Copper wire

1.5 volt battery

❓How do batteries make electricity?

There are metals and other special chemicals inside a battery, which can change to make electricity. The chemicals are dangerous, though, so never open a battery to look at them.

TRUE OR FALSE?

A lemon can be a battery.

TRUE. If you stick copper wire and a steel paper clip in a lemon, the metals will mix with the lemon juice and make electricity.

Spacecraft have batteries.

TRUE. The batteries make electricity for lights and machines.

❓How can I see sound?

Sound is a kind of energy which happens when something vibrates, or shakes, and makes the air around it vibrate as well. The vibrations travel through the air into your ears, and you hear sounds. You can see sound energy if you sprinkle sugar on a drum and then hit it with a stick. The vibrations will make the sugar shake up and down.

?How do sounds travel along telephone wires?

Telephones have a microphone in them which changes sound energy into electricity. The electricity flows through wires to another telephone, where a small speaker changes the electricity back into sound energy.

TRUE OR FALSE?

All phones need wires.

FALSE. Mobile phones change sound energy into radio signals, which can travel a long way without wires.

You can't hear sounds underwater.

FALSE. Sounds can travel through water and all sorts of other materials.

?Do magnets have glue in them?

No, magnets work because they have an invisible force called magnetism. Most magnets are made of iron or steel, and their magnetism pulls objects made of iron or steel towards them.

?How do magnets push and pull?

The two ends of a magnet are called its north and south poles. If you have two magnets, the north pole of one will attract (pull) the south pole of the other towards it. Two north poles or two south poles will repel (push) each other away.

?How do magnets help explorers?

Magnets are used in compasses because if a magnet can move freely, its north pole will always swing round to point towards the Earth's North Pole. You can test this out by hanging a bar magnet on a piece of string.

Magnet lines up with north.

NORTH

TRUE OR FALSE?

The Earth is a magnet.

TRUE. Its south magnetic pole is near the North Pole, and its north magnetic pole is near the South Pole.

Your fingers will stick to a magnet.

FALSE. Only iron or steel objects will stick to a magnet.

? Why are slides slippery?

Friction is a slowing force which happens when two surfaces rub against each other. Rough surfaces create stronger friction than smooth ones do, which is why slides are given smooth slippery surfaces. Can you imagine how difficult it would be to slide down a rough concrete ramp?

Front view
of brakes

Rubber block

Wheel

❓*Why do bikes have brakes?*

Brakes help a bike to stop, of course – but do you know why? It's because brakes use friction. When you squeeze the brakes, rubber blocks press against the wheels. The friction between the blocks and the wheels slows your bike down.

Friction helps you walk.

TRUE. Friction between your shoes and the ground helps you to grip and move forward.

The first bikes didn't have brakes.

TRUE. When the earliest bicycles were made in the 1790s, they didn't have brakes or pedals.

? Why do I fall over?

You might start to fall because you trip, but it's the invisible force of gravity that makes you end up on the ground. Gravity is a real downer – it's what tugs everything on Earth towards the ground and stops things like footballs from flying off into Space.

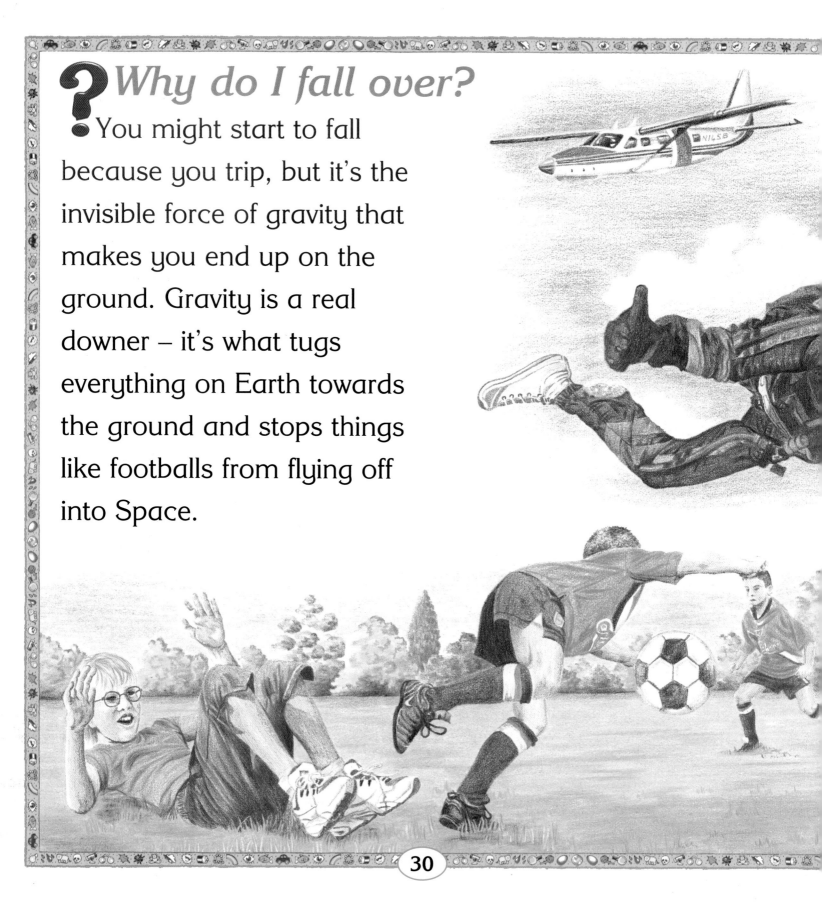

How fast do skydivers fall?

When skydivers jump out of an aeroplane they drop towards the ground at about 190 kph. Opening a parachute slows the skydiver down to about 20 kph – but that's still a lot faster than you can run!

What makes things heavy?

Gravity does! Weight is the effect of gravity on an object's mass – the amount of stuff it's made of. The more mass something has, the more gravity tugs it down and the heavier it is.

TRUE OR FALSE?

The Moon has no gravity.

FALSE. Like everything in the Universe, the Moon has gravity. It's about one-sixth of the Earth's.

Elephants are the heaviest animals.

FALSE. Blue whales can weigh 140 tonnes, which is heavier than 25 elephants.

Index